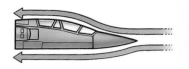

THE USBORNE BOOK OF
CUTAWAY
PLANES

Clive Gifford

Designed by Steve Page

Illustrated by: Sean Wilkinson, Robert Walster, Ian Cleaver, Mark Franklin and artists from the School of Illustration, Bournemouth and Poole College of Art and Design.

Series Editor: Cheryl Evans

Usborne Publishing wish to thank the following for their help with this book:

Airbus Industrie • Aircraft Research Association • Air International • Trevor Alner • British Aerospace Flying College Ltd. • Les Coombs • CSE Aviation • David Ditcher • Evans and Sutherland Computer Corporation • Flight Refuelling Ltd. • Helmet Integrated Systems • Hughes Corporation • Irvin GB Ltd. • Stephen Lake • Anthony Lawrence • Lord Corporation • Magellan Systems • Martin Baker Aircraft Company Ltd. • Martin Cross • Lockheed Martin Corporation • Michael Leek • Michelin • National Aerospace Laboratory (NLR) • Quadrant Picture Library • Stuart Priest • Richard Goode Aerobatic Displays • RFD Ltd. • Rolls-Royce Commercial Aero Engines Limited • Chris Sargent • SAS Flight Academy • Sextant Avionique • SFIM Industries • Clive Thomas • Thomson Training & Simulation • Steve Upson • Westland Aerospace

Contents

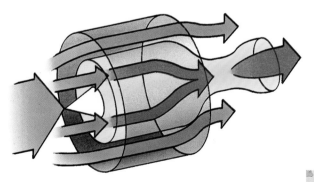

Words in *italic* type

Words which appear in *italic* type and are followed by a small star (for example, *friction**) can be found in the glossary on page 31.

Introduction

The first successful flights people ever made were with the help of balloons filled with gases to make them lighter than air. It was not until 1903 that two Americans, the Wright Brothers, found a way to fly a craft that was heavier than air. In the time since the Wright Brothers' first flight, many advances and inventions have made modern planes look very different from early ones.

BAe Hawk 200

This is a single-seat jet fighter designed by computer with many of the latest advances in aircraft design. Its top speed is almost 1,045km/h (650mph) and when it is empty it weighs only a little more than four family cars.

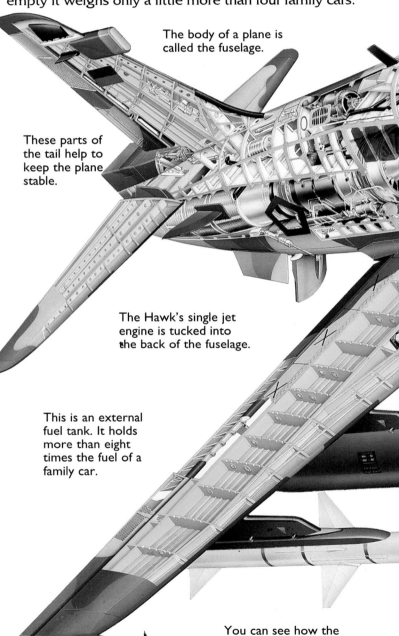

The body of a plane is called the fuselage.

These parts of the tail help to keep the plane stable.

The Hawk's single jet engine is tucked into the back of the fuselage.

This is an external fuel tank. It holds more than eight times the fuel of a family car.

You can see how the wing is made up of lots of strips all joined together. This makes the wing strong but much lighter than if it were made out of solid metal.

The Hawk 200's wingtips each hold a weapon called a Sidewinder missile.

The back edge of a wing is called the trailing edge.

The place where the pilot sits and flies the plane is called the cockpit.

A plane's wings are measured from one wingtip to the other. This is called the wingspan. The Hawk 200's wingspan is 9.9m (33ft).

The front edge of a wing is called the leading edge.

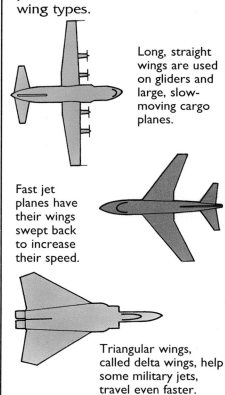

This is a two seater version of the Hawk, used by British display team, the Red Arrows.

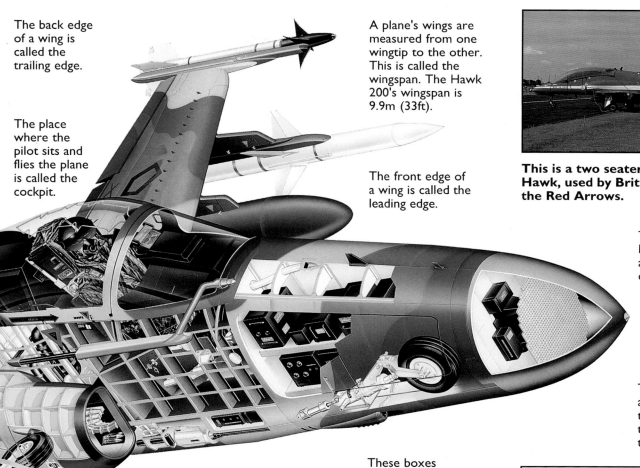

The nose of the Hawk contains advanced radar equipment.

This nosewheel and the wheels at the back are together called the landing gear.

This is an air intake. It channels air into the plane's jet engine. You can learn how a jet engine works on pages 10-11.

These boxes contain complicated electronics which help fly the aircraft. They are called avionics.

Wings

Wings are vital to planes. They provide the lift which takes the aircraft off the ground and into the air. They do this because of their specially curved shape.

As the engines pull the plane through the air, the leading edge of the wing divides the air, forcing some under it and some over. Both the top and bottom surfaces of the wing are curved but the top curves more steeply. The air moving over the wing, therefore has farther to go to catch up with the air moving underneath.

Slower-moving air presses more on the bottom of the wing than the faster moving air passing over the top of it. This stronger *air pressure** under the wing lifts it up.

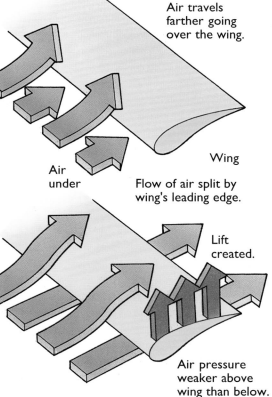

Air travels farther going over the wing.

Air under

Wing

Flow of air split by wing's leading edge.

Lift created.

Air pressure weaker above wing than below.

Wing types

There are many different wing shapes and sizes. Each type is best for a particular kind of plane. Here are three common wing types.

Long, straight wings are used on gliders and large, slow-moving cargo planes.

Fast jet planes have their wings swept back to increase their speed.

Triangular wings, called delta wings, help some military jets, travel even faster.

Controlling a plane

On the previous pages you saw how wings create lift. Lift is one of the *four forces of flight**. The others are thrust, drag and gravity. You can think of these four forces in pairs. For a plane to fly, lift must be greater than gravity, and thrust must be greater than drag.

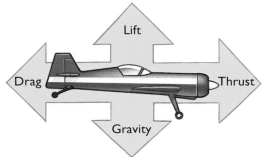

An aircraft uses its engines to create thrust and its wings to create lift. Modern planes are carefully designed to have less drag (see pages 14-15).

Control surfaces

Once in the air, a plane must be controlled otherwise it will crash. The plane must be kept balanced but also be able to change direction.

Changing direction is done by moving hinged parts of the wing, called ailerons, and hinged parts of the tail called the elevators and rudder. Together, these are known as control surfaces. Control surfaces change the direction of some of the air flowing around the plane. The change in the airflow changes the way the plane moves.

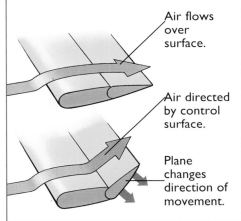

Air flows over surface.

Air directed by control surface.

Plane changes direction of movement.

This cutaway picture of a Slingsby Firefly shows the control surfaces and how they are linked to the controls in the cockpit.

The large hinged flap on both wings is called an aileron. It controls the rolling movement of the plane (see below left).

Small planes not used by the military are called light aircraft.

Rudder control cables

This hinged flap on the back of the tail is the rudder. It helps control the yawing movement (see below).

This hinged surface on the tail is called an elevator. It helps control the pitching movement (see below).

Roll

Roll is when you move the wings up and down using the ailerons. For example, turning the left aileron down will push the left wing up, pushing the right wing down.

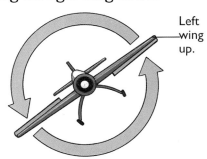

Left wing up.

Pitch

Pitch is when you move the fuselage up and down using the elevators. For example, turning the elevators down, lifts the tail up, causing the plane to dive down.

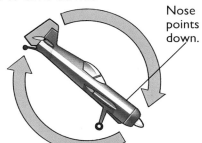

Nose points down.

Yaw

Yaw is when the plane moves from side to side. It is controlled by using the rudder. For example, turning the rudder left, will turn the plane's nose to the left.

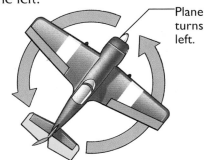

Plane turns left.

The Slingsby Firefly is made of modern materials. The rudder, for example, is made of plastic reinforced, or strengthened, with fine strands of glass.

This control column works two sets of control surfaces. Pushing it to the right and left moves the ailerons. Pushing it back and forth moves the elevators.

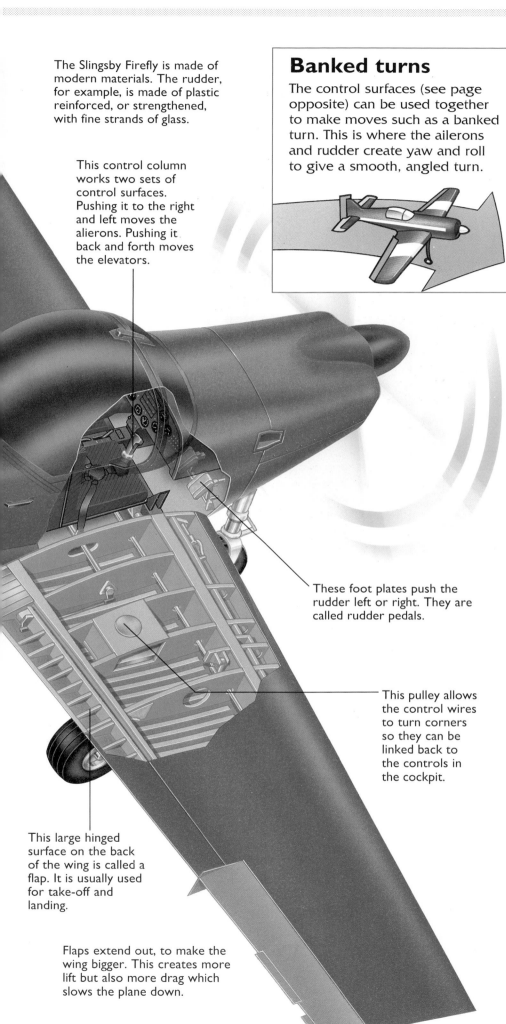

These foot plates push the rudder left or right. They are called rudder pedals.

This pulley allows the control wires to turn corners so they can be linked back to the controls in the cockpit.

This large hinged surface on the back of the wing is called a flap. It is usually used for take-off and landing.

Flaps extend out, to make the wing bigger. This creates more lift but also more drag which slows the plane down.

Banked turns

The control surfaces (see page opposite) can be used together to make moves such as a banked turn. This is where the ailerons and rudder create yaw and roll to give a smooth, angled turn.

Stalling

When a plane climbs, it is angled up and the air flows less smoothly over the wings. If an aircraft tries to climb too steeply without enough power, there is not enough speed for the air to flow over the wings and create lift. The flow of air breaks up and the aircraft begins to fall out of the sky. This is called *stalling**.

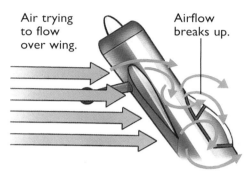

Air trying to flow over wing.

Airflow breaks up.

Pilots are taught how not to stall and how to recover if they do, but it can still be dangerous if the plane is near the ground. Modern planes have a complex set of sensors to help prevent stalling which is called a stall warning system.

Other surfaces

In addition to elevators, ailerons and a rudder, most modern planes have other control surfaces such as spoilers and slats. Slats do a similar job to flaps (see labels just to the left). They extend forward from the front, or leading edge, of the wing. Spoilers are large panels built into the wing which can lift up and 'spoil' the flow of air over the wing. They create less lift and more drag. They are used either to increase the effect of the ailerons or as air brakes (see page 19) to slow the aircraft down.

This airliner wing has its control surfaces arranged for just before landing.

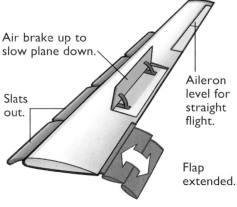

Air brake up to slow plane down.

Slats out.

Aileron level for straight flight.

Flap extended.

Cockpits

The cockpit is where the pilot sits and controls the aircraft. Instruments show how various parts of the plane are performing while navigation systems such as radar (see page 26) and the artificial horizon help keep it on the correct route.

The Optica's cockpit gives a clear view all the way around. It is ideal for aerial observation and photography.

Early cockpits

Early cockpits were often very uncomfortable. Many were open-air and left the pilot and any passengers unprotected from the weather.

A modern aircraft cockpit is full of controls and instruments, but the cockpits of the first planes were empty in comparison. You can see how simple an early aircraft's cockpit is by looking at the one in a 1933 De Havilland Leopard Moth (see right).

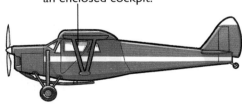

The Leopard Moth did have an enclosed cockpit.

There were 133 De Havilland Leopard Moths built in the 1930s.

From cockpit to wing

In gliders and light aircraft, the cockpit controls are linked directly to the *control surfaces** by a system of cables and pulleys.

In bigger aircraft, they have *hydraulic** systems instead of mechanical cables. Hydraulic power is created by putting a liquid under great pressure, as the diagram on the right shows. A liquid which doesn't freeze, even in very cold weather, is used to fill the cylinders and pipes of a hydraulic system.

Artificial Horizon

The artificial horizon tells the pilot if the plane is flying level. A gyroscope (see page 26) keeps a line on the dial exactly parallel with the horizon of the Earth. This line is the artificial horizon. When the aircraft tips one way or the other, the markings that show the plane's wings dip to either side of the horizon line.

For example, when the aircraft does a banked turn (see page 5) the horizon line appears to tilt. In fact, it remains parallel with the horizon of the Earth and the rest of the plane (including the wings on the dial) tilt around it.

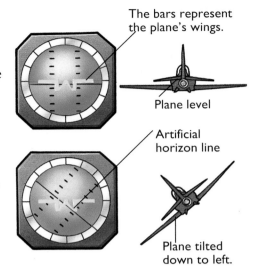

The bars represent the plane's wings.

Plane level

Artificial horizon line

Plane tilted down to left.

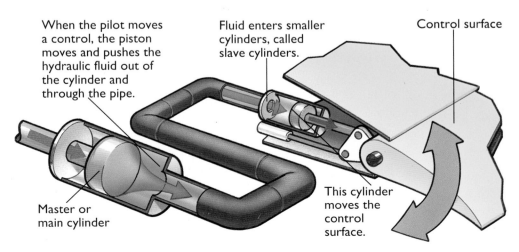

Thermometer

Altimeter (see right).

This is the plane's airspeed indicator (see right).

Control column

When the pilot moves a control, the piston moves and pushes the hydraulic fluid out of the cylinder and through the pipe.

Fluid enters smaller cylinders, called slave cylinders.

Control surface

Master or main cylinder

This cylinder moves the control surface.

Pitot tube and airspeed indicator

The pitot tube is a small tube mounted on the wing or body of the aircraft. It measures two types of *air pressure**: the pressure of the air around it, called static air pressure, and the pressure of the air rushing at it as the plane flies, called ram pressure. This information is fed into the aircraft's instruments.

A plane's speed through the air is shown by the airspeed indicator, or ASI. The relationship between the two air pressure readings from the pitot tube is changed by the ASI into the airspeed of the aircraft.

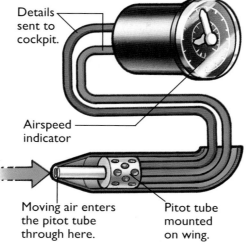

Details sent to cockpit.

Airspeed indicator

Moving air enters the pitot tube through here.

Pitot tube mounted on wing.

Altimeter

The altimeter tells the pilot the altitude, or height above ground, of the plane. Some altimeters use radar (see page 26) but others use the static pressure reading from the pitot tube. *Air pressure** gets less the higher you fly, so the altimeter can calculate the plane's height from the surrounding air pressure.

This sealed capsule of air helps the altimeter make its reading.

Modern cockpits

As aircraft became more advanced, the numbers of controls and instruments increased and cockpits became much more complicated.

Advanced airliners such as the Boeing 777 and Airbus A340 have their cockpits, called flight decks, specially designed to be simpler and better laid out than before. The cockpit of the A340 (shown on the left) has computer screens which display different types of information, instead of rows of individual instruments.

Here is a test model of the A340 airliner on the ground at the Farnborough Airshow in England.

The throttles control the speed of the engines.

Fly by wire joystick (see below).

Pilot's seat

Co-pilot's seat

Fly-by-wire

In the very latest aircraft, some hydraulic systems are replaced with an advanced system called fly-by-wire. With fly-by-wire, electric wires run from a computer to a mixture of electric motors and small hydraulic systems called *actuators** in the wings and tail. When the pilot moves the controls, signals from the computer instruct the motors and hydraulics to move the control surfaces. Fly-by-wire is very precise, much lighter and easier to repair than hydraulics and works well with the plane's flight computers.

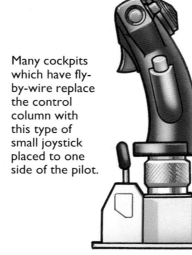

Many cockpits which have fly-by-wire replace the control column with this type of small joystick placed to one side of the pilot.

The General Dynamics F16 Fighting Falcon was one of the first military jets to feature fly-by-wire controls.

Airliners

Airliners are planes that carry large numbers of passengers. The earliest airliners carried just a few people and were cold and noisy. These planes could only travel long distances by making small hops from place to place.

This Ford Tri-motor had a maximum range of just over 800km (500 miles). Some of today's airliners can fly 20 times as far without having to refuel.

Airbus A340-300 and -200

The A340 is the latest in a line of airliners built by several European companies working together under the name Airbus Industrie. There are two versions of the A340. The -300 (shown below) has a long *range** but the -200 can travel even farther. The -200's fuselage is 4m (13ft) shorter and the plane has fewer seats but more fuel. In 1993, an Airbus A340-200 flew around the world stopping only once, in New Zealand, to refuel. The whole journey took just over 48 hours.

Here's an Airbus A340-300 test aircraft in flight.

Airliner fuselages must be incredibly strong to withstand the pressure of high altitude flight and protect the passengers and crew inside.

This is one of the A340's eight passenger exits.

Here is the inner shell of the airliner's fuselage.

Pressurization

As a plane flies higher and higher, the air around it gets thinner. At the altitudes a modern jet airliner flies, there is not enough air for the passengers to breathe. What they do is to keep the airliner's airtight fuselage filled with *pressurized** air that the passengers and crew can breathe normally.

The top floor or deck holds the passengers. It is called the cabin.

Here you can see the complicated structure of the wing.

These air brakes are positioned up to slow the airliner down. You can learn more about air brakes on page 19.

On the ground the pressure of the air inside the plane is the same as the air outside it.

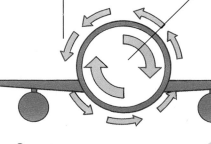

At great heights, the air has less pressure and is much thinner.

In flight, the air inside the plane is kept to a similar pressure to the air on the ground.

Wing rib

Because of concerns about the environment, new airliners' engines have to be cleaner and quieter than before.

Fan blades

This wingtip angled up is called a winglet. It helps make the A340 more stable.

Passenger configurations

The number of seats, what type they are and the way they are arranged inside an airliner is called the passenger configuration. Cheaper seats are squeezed together so airliners can carry more people, but business or luxury seats have more room. A plane's passenger configuration can be changed easily.

Here you can see the numbers of seats across the plane's body in different classes.

Six seats across in first or luxury class.

Seven seats across in business class.

Eight seats across in economy class.

These are the business class seats.

Luxury or first class seats.

Sitting comfortably

Airlines are always trying to make their passengers more comfortable. New ideas include seats that convert into beds so that the passenger can sleep and individual video screens in front of each passenger.

Computer

A business class seat of the future may have its own computer and fax machine.

The lower floor is the luggage or cargo hold.

You can see the A340's flight deck on page 7.

All the other staff in the plane, apart from the pilot, are called aircrew.

Loading and unloading

All airliners carry some cargo, from the passenger's suitcases to mail and packages. When they land, many airliners have to unload the passengers, crew and cargo and also be checked, filled with fuel and then loaded again for another journey. This is called turning around an aircraft and it involves many people working together.

Inside the airport, Load Controllers decide the airliner's load, how it is placed around the plane and how much fuel the plane will need.

Cleaners clean the inside of the plane.

Cargo trucks carry baggage to and from the aircraft.

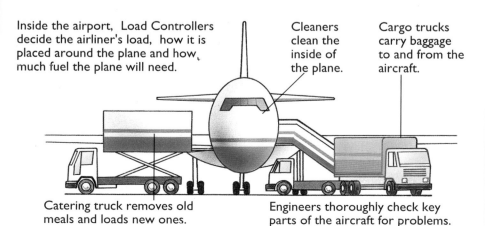

Catering truck removes old meals and loads new ones.

Engineers thoroughly check key parts of the aircraft for problems.

Cargo planes

Some airliners have been rebuilt to carry just cargo. The latest large cargo carrier is a new version of the Airbus A300 airliner, called the A300-600ST. It can carry enormous pieces of machinery or rocket and plane parts up to a weight of 45 metric tonnes (50 tons).

The A300-600ST's fuselage is over 7.2m (24ft) across.

Engines

All aircraft need one or more engines to push them forward. Many use piston engines to drive propellers. Fast military planes and modern airliners use jet, or turbine, engines.

Piston engines

The first piston engines were built for cars in the 1880s. Aircraft piston engines work in a similar way to those found in cars. Instead of driving wheels around though, an they spin a propeller at very high speeds. This propeller pulls the aircraft through the air. An aircraft engine is powered by a mixture of fuel and air injected into the engine's cylinders, where it is set alight and burned.

This is a simple diagram of a piston engine.

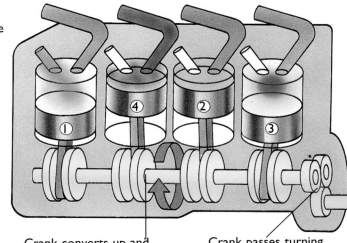

1. Air and fuel injected into cylinder.

2. Piston moves up cylinder squeezing air and fuel together

3. Mixture is burned to create gases which push piston down cylinder.

4. Piston moves up cylinder and pushes out waste gases.

Crank converts up and down movement of piston into a turning movement

Crank passes turning power via gears to the propeller shaft.

Turbine engines

A turbine engine burns fuel and air, a little like a piston engine, but instead of moving a piston up and down, it drives a series of fan blades, called a turbine, around at high speeds. Turbine engines were first used to power aircraft in World War II. There are many different types of turbine engines. The most common is the turbofan engine. These are found on jet airliners, military cargo transporters and many other types of jet aircraft.

Rolls Royce RB211-535

This is a large and powerful turbofan engine built by the British company, Rolls Royce. One engine alone produces 19,200kg (42,100lbs) of thrust, more power than fifty family cars can produce. It is fitted to several modern jet airliners such as the Russian Tupolev Tu204.

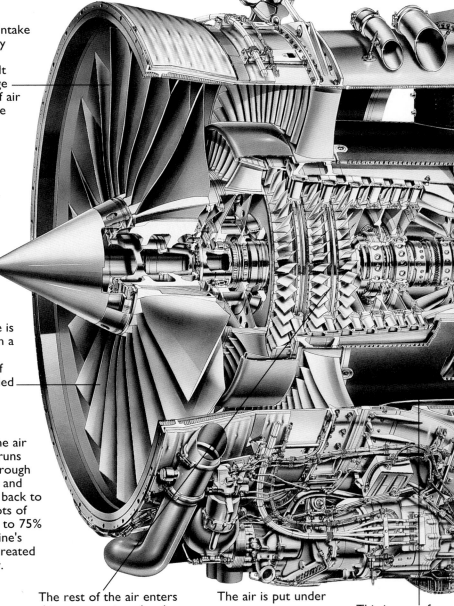

This large intake fan is a very efficient propeller. It pushes huge amounts of air through the engine.

The fan is just over 2m (74in) across.

Each blade is made from a complex mixture of metals called an alloy.

Much of the air sucked in runs straight through the engine and out of the back to produce lots of thrust. Up to 75% of the engine's power is created in this way.

The rest of the air enters this compression chamber where it is squeezed together by sets of fans.

The air is put under enormous pressure, over 30 times as much as normal.

This is one of the engine's bypass ducts.

This Boeing 757 is powered by two RB211-535 engines.

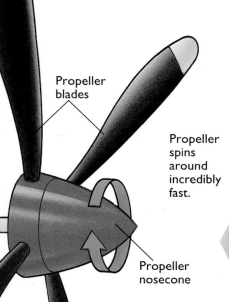

Propeller blades

Propeller spins around incredibly fast.

Propeller nosecone

Propellers

Propellers are made up of between two and five blades. These are shaped to cut through the air and push it backwards. Pushing the air backwards has the effect of pulling the aircraft forwards. The angle of each blade is called the propeller's pitch.

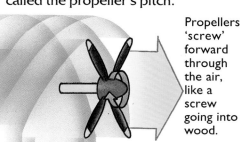

Propellers 'screw' forward through the air, like a screw going into wood.

Many propellers have variable pitch. This means that they can change the angle of their blades for different flying jobs and situations. For example, a steep climb may need more sharp pulling power whilst cruising on the level needs less.

Propellers can have different numbers of blades. This Russian Antonov An76 research aircraft has propellers with 12 blades.

Fuel is injected into the combustion chamber and mixed with the air.

The fuel and air mixture is ignited and burns at almost 1500°C (2700°F).

Burning the fuel and air creates hot expanding gases which turn these combustion turbines.

The blades on these turbines revolve at speeds as fast as 10,000 turns a minute. They create a great deal of power.

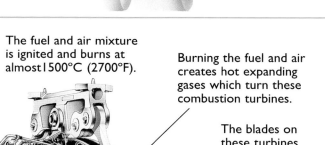

A lot of the engine's power is taken along this shaft and used to drive the intake fan and the turbines in the compression chamber.

The remaining power is pushed out of the back of the engine to create more thrust.

The compressed air enters this combustion chamber.

Turbojets and props

Turbojets are the simplest type of turbine engine. Thrust is only provided by the hot gases being pushed out of the back of the engine. Turbojets give very high speeds but tend to be noisy and use a lot of fuel. They are found on some fast modern jet aircraft.

Concorde is powered by four Olympus 593 turbojet engines.

Turboprop engines have an extra turbine which uses much of the thrust created by the engine to drive a propeller. Turboprops burn less fuel and are much quieter than other turbine engines but cannot fly faster than about 800km/h (500mph).

Splitting the air

Air sucked in at the front of a turbofan engine is split. Some enters the core of the engine where it helps burn fuel to produce thrust. However, as much as ten times that amount of air bypasses the middle and flows through the engine's bypass ducts. This air creates much more thrust and also helps cool the engine core.

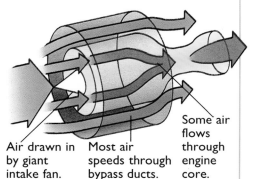

Air drawn in by giant intake fan.

Most air speeds through bypass ducts.

Some air flows through engine core.

This Fokker F27 has two turboprops.

Aircraft constuction

The very first planes were built from materials that were easily available and were quite light. Certain types of light wood were used as a skeleton which was then covered with cloth stretched tight.

Although these planes were light enough to be lifted into the air by the weak engines they had at the time, they were not very strong.

LVG CVI

This German LVG CVI two-seat bomber was built near the end of World War One. By that time, advances in aircraft design had helped to make planes less flimsy. For its time, the LVG CVI was a strong plane, but heavy and quite slow.

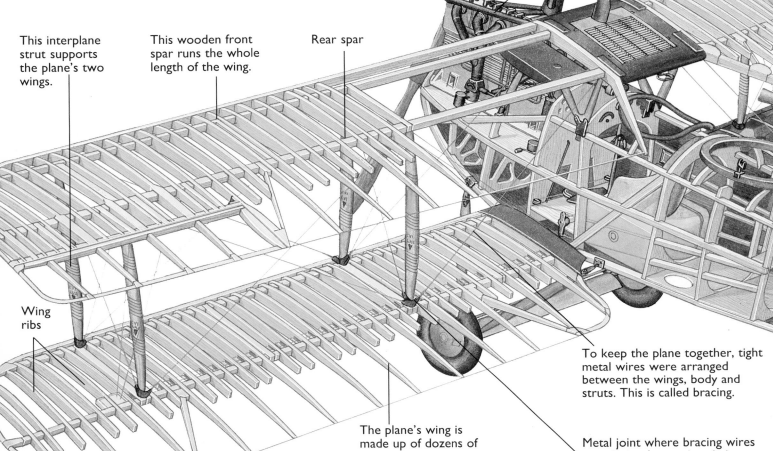

The engine produced almost as much power as three modern family car engines. Yet, because of its weight and shape, it's top speed was only 170km/h (105mph).

This interplane strut supports the plane's two wings.

This wooden front spar runs the whole length of the wing.

Rear spar

Wing ribs

To keep the plane together, tight metal wires were arranged between the wings, body and struts. This is called bracing.

The plane's wing is made up of dozens of wooden ribs.

Metal joint where bracing wires joined plane's wooden skeleton.

Advances in aircraft structure

After World War One, planes began to be built using more metal. Many plane makers used metal or thin sheets of wood instead of the outer covering of fabric. They also used tough metal steel tubing instead of wood for the inner skeleton.

The design of planes changed greatly as *duralumin**, a metal *alloy**, began to be made in sheets. Duralumin was used to make a stressed metal skin which was strong but lighter than large parts of the inner skeleton which it replaced.

Other metal alloys have since been invented which are stronger or lighter than duralumin, or are more heat resistant. Some of these contain a metal called titanium which is very strong and has an extremely high melting point.

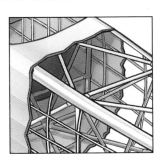

Here you can see part of the steel tube framework of an American, Curtiss Hawk plane.

This German BF109G has a stressed skin shell called a monocoque.

Many parts of this Sukhoi Su26 are made from advanced metal alloys.

This bright design, printed onto the cloth that covers the wing, is called a lozenge pattern.

The LVG CVI carried a pilot and a rear gunner who also aimed the plane's small bomb load.

The plane's body and wings were covered with a light cloth. This was then varnished to make the cloth fit tightly over the wooden frame.

The structure of the tailfin is quite simple.

These long struts run the length of the fuselage and are called longerons.

These fuselage body frames use a lot of wood.

Wires for rudder control.

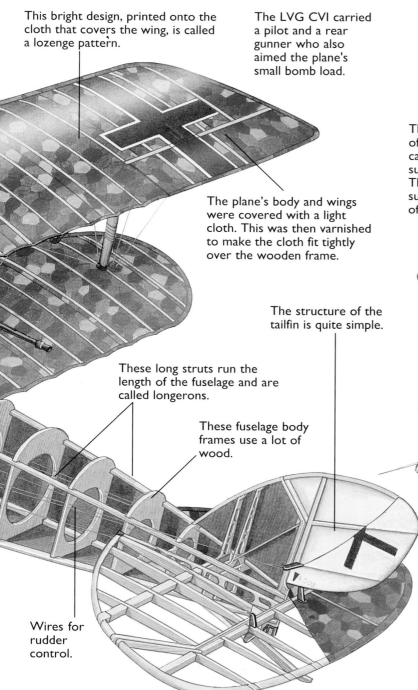

Modern aircraft building

Like modern cars, planes are made from thousands of parts which are all made and tested separately, before being put together into bigger sections. The framework of the plane is built and then the moving parts and electronics are added.

The solid frame of the aircraft is called the superstructure. This is the superstructure of a BAe Hawk.

Rudder will attach to back of tail.

Wing rib

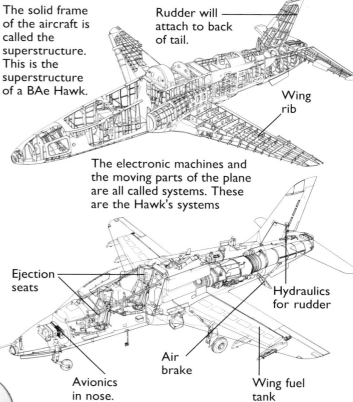

The electronic machines and the moving parts of the plane are all called systems. These are the Hawk's systems

Ejection seats

Hydraulics for rudder

Air brake

Avionics in nose.

Wing fuel tank

Composites

Composites are materials made of millions of thin strands of man-made materials all bonded together by an incredibly strong adhesive. They are very strong and light. Advanced composites, such as Kevlar, are being used more and more in aircraft building.

This flap from a Slingsby Firefly has a covering of Kevlar sheet.

Computer Aided Design

This computer is helping design a Rolls Royce engine.

Computer Aided Design (CAD) uses powerful computers that allow engineers to experiment with and accurately design aircraft parts on-screen. Once the design is decided upon, other computers simulate extreme conditions such as cold, heat, wear and stress, to test these parts thoroughly.

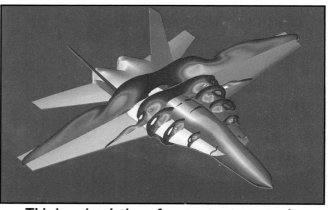

This is a simulation of computer tests made on a military jet's structure.

Aerodynamics and fuel

Aerodynamics is the study of how a moving object travels through a liquid or a gas, such as air. It is vital to know how planes fly for lots of reasons. When a plane moves forward, the air flows over the wings which creates lift. When the air flows over the *control surfaces**, it allows the plane to change direction. When air flows over the whole plane, it creates drag. Drag slows a plane down and makes it use more fuel. Changing the shape and surface of a plane to reduce drag is called *streamlining**.

Box shape

Air flow

Air hits flat front of plane and cannot pass by easily. This creates lots of drag.

Air flows smoothly around a modern jet.

Concorde's delta wing shape was carefully designed to create the maximum amount of lift with as little drag as possible.

As many as 128 passenger seats can be squeezed close together.

G-BOAA

Concorde

Concorde is the fastest airliner in the world with a top speed of 2300km/h (1430mph), more than twice the speed of other modern airliners. Concorde is so fast mainly because of its incredibly powerful engines and its advanced aerodynamic shape which is very streamlined.

This is the galley where food is prepared.

British airways

The pointed nose helps cut through the air.

The flight deck seats three people.

Twin nosewheels

The fuselage is long and thin with a smooth, rounded shape. This makes it more streamlined.

Here you can see the complicated structure of the wing which is needed to make it strong while keeping it light.

The nose stays straight when flying but drops down to let the pilot see better for take-off and landing.

Concorde has been carefully streamlined so that few parts stick out from its smooth shape.

Concorde's cruising speed means it flies 10km (6 miles) every 15 seconds.

Advances in streamlining

Early aircraft with lots of struts and wires made no real attempts at streamlining, but as planes got faster and exceeded 200km/h (125mph) streamlining became more important. Gradually, the number of struts and wires holding a plane together was reduced and the ones that were left were shaped to help the air flow more smoothly around them. Engines which had been left out in the open were later put inside smoothly-shaped engine covers which are called cowlings.

Engine cowling

Air flows smoothly past.

Monoplanes with one set of wings, which needed almost no struts or bracing, started to replace *biplanes** during the twenties and thirties. Fixed landing gears were replaced with retractable ones (see page 18). These could be lowered for take-off and landing and raised to create much less drag when flying.

With the arrival of jet engines, aircraft could travel much faster and this called for more changes in the shape of aircraft. Their surfaces were made as smooth as possible. The front of planes became sharper to cut through the air, and wings were swept back to make the aircraft even more streamlined.

The Supermarine Spitfire was among the first military planes to have a retractable landing gear.

The Hawker Hunter's swept back wings helped it reach a top speed of over 1100km/h (690mph).

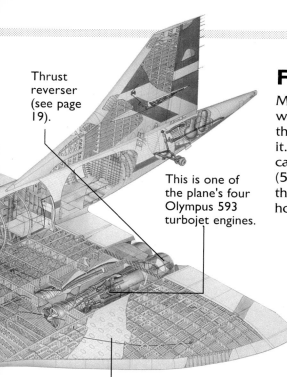

Thrust reverser (see page 19).

This is one of the plane's four Olympus 593 turbojet engines.

Concorde flies high where the air may be colder than -60°C (-76°F). These de-icing panels stop ice from forming on the wings which can reduce lift.

Fuel

Modern aircraft, especially those with jet engines, use fuel so quickly they have to carry huge amounts of it. A Boeing 747, for example, can carry as much as 197,000 litres (52,000 gallons) of fuel. Compare that to a typical family car which holds only 70 litres (15 gallons).

A plane must stay balanced as it flies. As fuel is used up, the balance of a plane changes. Many modern aircraft have *fuel management systems**. These measure how much fuel is in each tank and can switch which tank supplies fuel at any time, to even up their weight.

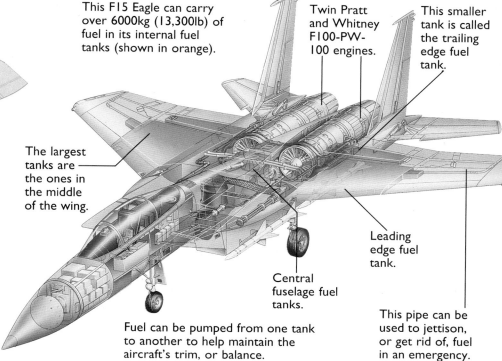

This F15 Eagle can carry over 6000kg (13,300lb) of fuel in its internal fuel tanks (shown in orange).

Twin Pratt and Whitney F100-PW-100 engines.

This smaller tank is called the trailing edge fuel tank.

The largest tanks are the ones in the middle of the wing.

Leading edge fuel tank.

Central fuselage fuel tanks.

This pipe can be used to jettison, or get rid of, fuel in an emergency.

Fuel can be pumped from one tank to another to help maintain the aircraft's trim, or balance.

Wind Tunnel

As scientists and engineers have learned more and more about aerodynamics, they have been able to build planes that fly faster, farther and more safely. The most useful and important way to study aerodynamics has been in a wind tunnel.

Even the very earliest planes were first tested as scale models inside simple wind tunnels. Wind tunnels today are much more complicated but the principles are still the same. Air is blown over a scale model of the aircraft, or part of it, and engineers see the effect this has. Computers are used to monitor results.

This airliner model is being tested in a high speed wind tunnel.

Adding fuel in-flight

The plane's fuel tank is usually filled on the ground where tanker trucks pump fuel into the tanks at incredibly fast speeds.

Some military planes, though, can take on extra fuel while flying. A large tanker aircraft, often a converted airliner or cargo plane, flies close to the plane in need of fuel. This requires great skill from both pilots.

This VC10 tanker can supply planes with up to 86,000kg (190,000lb) of fuel through its three fuel probes.

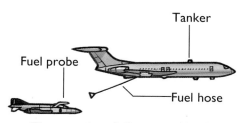

Tanker

Fuel probe

Fuel hose

The two aircraft fly extremely close to each other. The tanker extends its hose, the other plane extends its fuel probe.

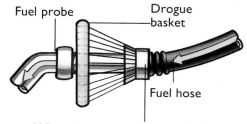

Fuel probe

Drogue basket

Fuel hose

When the two probes join, fuel is pumped quickly from the tanker to the plane that needs fuel.

Learning to fly

These trainees at a flying school are being taught about radio communications.

Becoming a pilot takes a long time and lots of hard work. This is because pilots have to know so much information about the aircraft they fly and about other important things, such as weather, maintainance, safety and navigation. Trainee pilots are tested on many lessons in the classroom as well as flying with an instructor in an aircraft called a trainer.

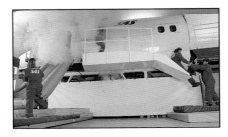

Aircrew, as well as pilots, need training. Here, aircrew learn what to do if there's a fire.

Trainers

Trainers often have two sets of controls so that the instructor can take over if the trainee pilot is having difficulty. There are trainers for all different types of aircraft.

This Cessna 150 is a light plane trainer. It is one of the most common planes in the world.

Pilot and trainee sit side by side.

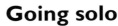

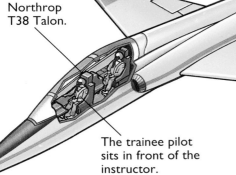

This is a Northrop T38 Talon.

The trainee pilot sits in front of the instructor.

The T38 is used to train American fighter pilots.

Going solo

After many hours in the classroom and up in the air with an instructor, a trainee pilot must fly the aircraft alone, without the instructor's help. This is called going solo. Once trainees have flown solo for a certain time, have learned about flying cross-country and passed various tests, they will be given their first pilot's licence.

Gliding

Some people learn to fly in a type of plane without an engine called a glider or sailplane. Learning to glide is cheaper and easier than learning to fly a powered aircraft but it is still extremely exciting and demanding.

Gliders can be launched into the air in many ways. A few gliders have small engines just for take-off. Many gliders are launched using a powerful winch on the ground. The winch pulls the glider along fast enough for the air rushing over the wings to provide the lift needed for take-off.

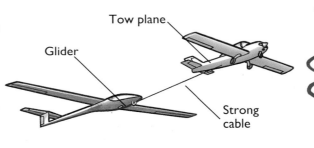

Tow plane

Glider

Strong cable

Thermals

Some gliders are towed into the air by a light aircraft known as a tug or tow plane. At an agreed height, the glider is released and the tow plane flies back to the airfield.

Once in the air, gliders circle around on pockets of warm air called thermals. An experienced pilot in good conditions can keep a glider flying for many hours.

T-shaped tail with the elevators on top of the tail fin.

Gliders are built from strong but very light materials to keep their weight down. These long wings provide lots of lift.

Single wheel landing gear

This glider's cockpit seats two people.

Aileron

Flight simulators

Flight simulators are complex machines which make you feel you are really flying. They do this by using a mixture of projector displays, realistic movement, and a complete copy of the real plane's cockpit. Flight simulators are not just flown by trainees. Experienced pilots also use them when learning to fly new aircraft or when working on how to cope with an emergency, which would be difficult or dangerous to do in a real aircraft.

This simulator is used by Japanese airline, JAL, to train their pilots.

Here is an example of the sort of realistic scene which can be generated by computers and viewed from inside an advanced simulator.

Aerobatics

Tricks and special moves performed by a pilot in a plane are called aerobatics. It takes a long time for even experienced pilots to learn how to do them.

This Pitts Special is a very rugged biplane often used for aerobatics.

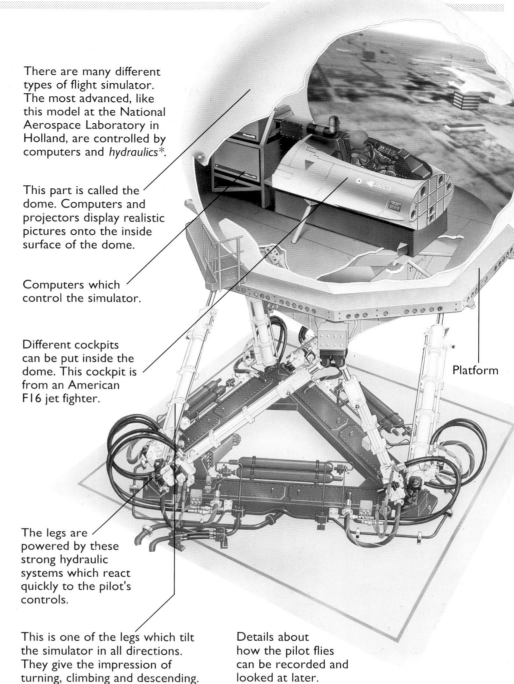

There are many different types of flight simulator. The most advanced, like this model at the National Aerospace Laboratory in Holland, are controlled by computers and *hydraulics**.

This part is called the dome. Computers and projectors display realistic pictures onto the inside surface of the dome.

Computers which control the simulator.

Different cockpits can be put inside the dome. This cockpit is from an American F16 jet fighter.

Platform

The legs are powered by these strong hydraulic systems which react quickly to the pilot's controls.

This is one of the legs which tilt the simulator in all directions. They give the impression of turning, climbing and descending.

Details about how the pilot flies can be recorded and looked at later.

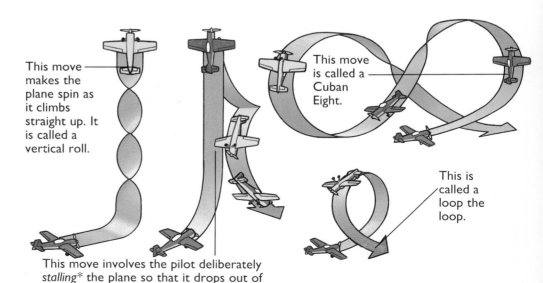

This move makes the plane spin as it climbs straight up. It is called a vertical roll.

This move is called a Cuban Eight.

This is called a loop the loop.

This move involves the pilot deliberately *stalling** the plane so that it drops out of the sky. It is called a stall turn.

Take-off and landing

Nearly all planes need a long stretch of flat ground or calm water for take-off and landing. Take-off and landing are a pilot's busiest times.

How a plane takes off

Taking off needs more power than any other part of a flight. A plane at take-off is at its heaviest because it hasn't used much of its fuel. The engines must move the plane fast enough for the wings to overcome the plane's weight and lift the plane into the sky. Below is a diagram of how a plane takes off and lands.

Floats and skids

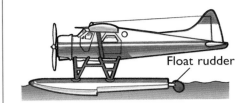

Float rudder

This Canadian DHC-2 Beaver can be fitted with floats or skids.

Some aircraft don't need a runway for take-off and landing. Their landing gear wheels (see below) may be replaced with skids for landing on ground; or replaced with floats, underneath their fuselage or wing, for landing on water. These floats usually have small rudders on the back to allow the pilot to steer the plane once it is on the water.

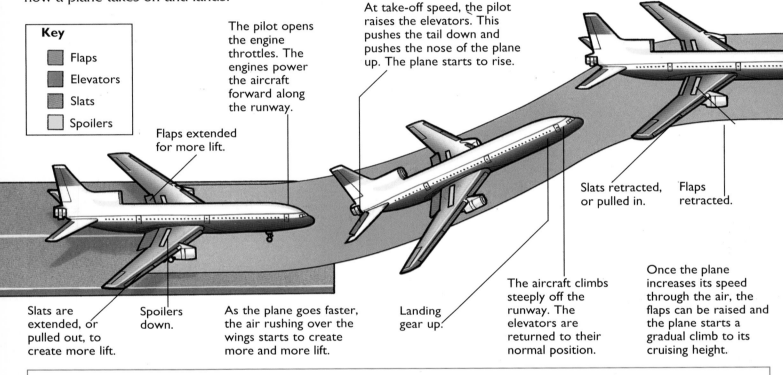

Key
- Flaps
- Elevators
- Slats
- Spoilers

The pilot opens the engine throttles. The engines power the aircraft forward along the runway.

At take-off speed, the pilot raises the elevators. This pushes the tail down and pushes the nose of the plane up. The plane starts to rise.

Flaps extended for more lift.

Slats retracted, or pulled in.

Flaps retracted.

Slats are extended, or pulled out, to create more lift.

Spoilers down.

As the plane goes faster, the air rushing over the wings starts to create more and more lift.

Landing gear up.

The aircraft climbs steeply off the runway. The elevators are returned to their normal position.

Once the plane increases its speed through the air, the flaps can be raised and the plane starts a gradual climb to its cruising height.

The landing gear

The parts of the plane that touch the ground at take-off and landing, and the parts that support them, are called the landing gear. As a plane lands, the landing gear is put under great strain. Modern landing gears are very strong. For example, the entire Boeing 747 landing gear is tested to support almost double the plane's actual weight, which is an incredible 360,000kg (800,000lb).

This is part of the landing gear of a Falcon 900 business jet.

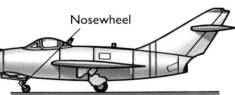

Nosewheel

The most most common form of landing gear has three sets of wheels and is called a tricycle landing gear. Both these planes have this sort of landing gear.

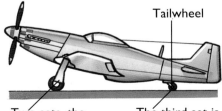

Tailwheel

Two sets, the main gear, are placed under the body or wings of the plane.

The third set is either under the nose or tail to keep the plane level.

Retractable landing gear first became common in the 1930s. It helps make the plane much more *streamlined*.

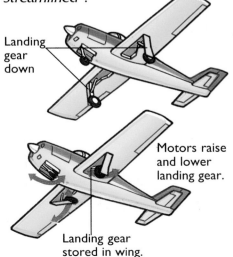

Landing gear down

Motors raise and lower landing gear.

Landing gear stored in wing.

How a plane lands

The pilot carefully sets a course to fly down to the runway. As the plane starts to descend, the pilot makes small changes to the position of the elevators and the power of the engines. When the plane is within 5 or 6m (16-20ft) of the ground, the pilot reduces engine power and raises the elevators a little more. The plane gently his the runway.

Take-off and landing at sea

On many aircraft carriers, a strong catapult driven by steam from the ship's boilers can pull an aircraft from a standstill to 240km/h (150mph) in under two seconds.

An arrester hook is fitted to many aircraft on ships. As the plane lands, the hook trails along the deck and catches on a strong set of cables which act as an anchor.

Slats and flaps out for extra lift.

Ideally, a plane lands into the wind. This cuts down the landing speed.

Once the plane is safely onto the runway, the pilot operates the wheel brakes to slow the aircraft down.

A modern airliner touches the runway at a speed of about 300km/h (180mph).

Landing gear down

The plane descends at a small angle. The pilot adjusts the throttles to keep the plane at a steady speed.

As the plane's wheels touch the runway, the pilot closes the throttle to cut the speed of the engines right down.

Spoilers raised which cuts down lift.

Stopping after landing

Modern aircraft land at high speeds. They have other methods, apart from the wheel brakes, to help them stop quickly.

Air brakes or spoilers can be on a planes's body or its wings (see page 5). They are flaps that open out to disrupt the flow of air. This creates plenty of drag which slows the aircraft down.

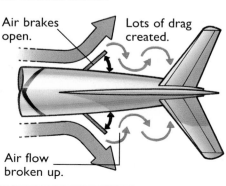

Air brakes open.

Lots of drag created.

Air flow broken up.

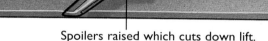
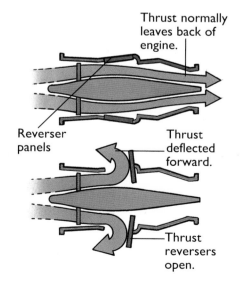

Thrust normally leaves back of engine.

Reverser panels

Thrust deflected forward.

Thrust reversers open.

Thrust reversers simply change the direction the engine's power is pushing. Instead of the power pushing the plane forward, it pushes against the way the plane is moving, so the plane slows down.

Some planes are fitted with brake parachutes. These open up from the back of the aircraft and create a lot of drag which helps slow the plane down. A brake parachute on a military jet fighter may take only two seconds to inflate fully but can cut 25% off the braking distance in dry conditions and as much as 50% in the wet.

This F117A stealth fighter has used its brake parachute on landing.

VSTOL planes

VSTOL stands for Vertical or Short Take-Off and Landing. A VSTOL plane can either use a short stretch of runway or can take off and land straight up and down from a small space such as a clearing in a forest or jungle. Much of the time, VSTOL planes use a runway for a short take-off but land vertically. This saves a lot of fuel.

This machine, called the Flying Bedstead, was built by Rolls Royce to test engines for VSTOL. It was first used in 1953.

BAe Sea Harrier Mk1

The Harrier is the best known VSTOL plane. It was first built by British company Hawker Siddeley (later British Aerospace) and Harriers have served in the British, Indian, Italian, Spanish and United States military services. The Sea Harrier is a version of the Harrier used by navies. It can take off and land from the decks of aircraft carriers and has a top speed of 1,120km/h (720mph).

This Sea Harrier is landing vertically onto the deck of an aircraft carrier.

The wing joins the very top of the fuselage. This is called a shoulder type wing.

This is the engine's front or intake fan.

Front exhaust nozzle (see below).

Advanced Blue Fox radar is stored in the nose.

This measures how much the plane yaws (see page 4). It is called a yaw vane.

The single pilot sits on a Martin Baker Type 10 ejection seat. He can eject safely even from the ship's deck.

Wedges called chocks stop the plane from moving when parked on the ground.

This external fuel tank holds more fuel than the tanks of 12 family cars.

Pegasus engine

The Harrier is powered by a single turbofan engine called the Rolls Royce Pegasus. The main difference between the Pegasus and other turbofans is that the direction the gases leave the engine can be controlled. This is called vectored thrust (see opposite page). The engine has four linked exhaust nozzles through which the hot gases and cold air are forced out. These nozzles can be turned around by the pilot from the cockpit.

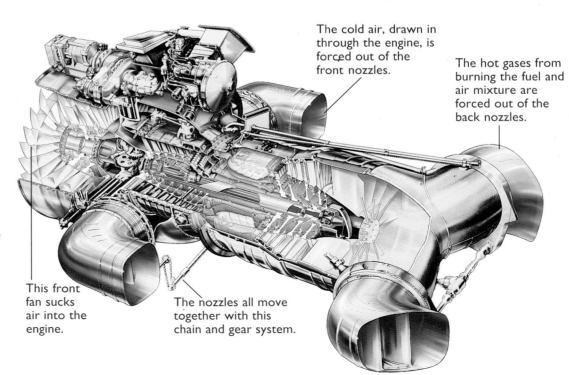

The cold air, drawn in through the engine, is forced out of the front nozzles.

The hot gases from burning the fuel and air mixture are forced out of the back nozzles.

This front fan sucks air into the engine.

The nozzles all move together with this chain and gear system.

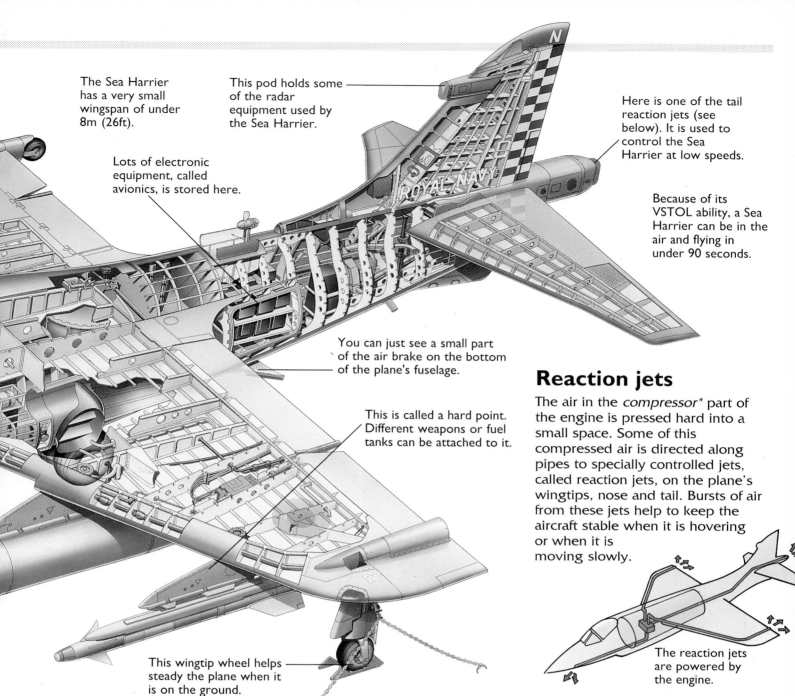

The Sea Harrier has a very small wingspan of under 8m (26ft).

This pod holds some of the radar equipment used by the Sea Harrier.

Here is one of the tail reaction jets (see below). It is used to control the Sea Harrier at low speeds.

Lots of electronic equipment, called avionics, is stored here.

Because of its VSTOL ability, a Sea Harrier can be in the air and flying in under 90 seconds.

You can just see a small part of the air brake on the bottom of the plane's fuselage.

This is called a hard point. Different weapons or fuel tanks can be attached to it.

This wingtip wheel helps steady the plane when it is on the ground.

Reaction jets

The air in the *compressor** part of the engine is pressed hard into a small space. Some of this compressed air is directed along pipes to specially controlled jets, called reaction jets, on the plane's wingtips, nose and tail. Bursts of air from these jets help to keep the aircraft stable when it is hovering or when it is moving slowly.

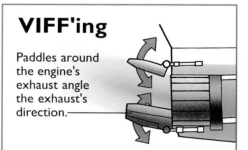

The reaction jets are powered by the engine.

Vectored thrust

Vectored thrust works by nozzles directing the flow of gases out of the engine. The engine can produce up to 88kN (19,800lb) of thrust. Most or all of this is needed for vertical take-off. If the plane weighs more than the thrust can lift straight up, it cannot take off vertically and must use a ramp or runway instead.

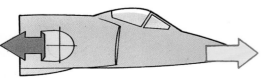

When the nozzles are set pointing back, the gases are forced back which powers the aircraft forward.

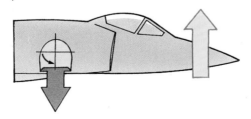

With the nozzles pointing down, the gases are forced down which provides up-thrust, lifting the plane off the ground.

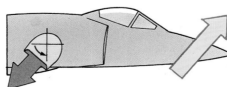

Angling the nozzles diagonally down moves the aircraft both up and forward at the same time.

VIFF'ing

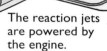

Paddles around the engine's exhaust angle the exhaust's direction.

Pilots can use vectored thrust while flying. By altering the direction of the exhaust, a plane can make tighter turns and climb faster than normal. This is called VIFF'ing (Vectoring In Forward Flight). Some military fighters which are not VSTOL aircraft are now being fitted with equipment which allows them to VIFF. This will make them faster and easier to move around in combat.

Safety

Early planes were often dangerous to fly. They were difficult to control and had few safety features or instruments to help the pilot. Modern aircraft are not only easier to control but also contain many instruments designed to avoid accidents. For example, radar warns of aircraft or other problems ahead.

The flight data recorder, often called the black box, records all the details of a flight.

The black box is examined by experts if there's a crash or other problem.

Passenger safety

Modern airliners are designed carefully to avoid accidents and can still fly even if one engine stops working. They all have many features built in to help passengers survive and escape from the plane if it crashes.

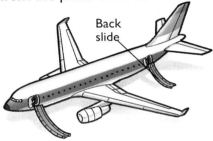

Back slide

These slides are a quick and safe way to leave the aircraft. They are filled with air and are worked by the airliner's aircrew.

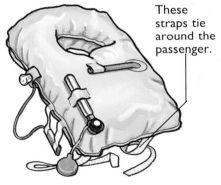

These straps tie around the passenger.

All passengers have a life jacket by or under their seats. They inflate automatically when you pull a tab.

Life rafts provide safety and shelter for survivors if a plane crashes in water. This raft, made by RFD Equipment, holds up to 9 people.

Ejection seats

Jet aircraft fly too fast for pilots and crew members to jump out of the plane and use a parachute. So an ejection seat is used to fire crew members safely out of the plane and away from danger.

Since they were introduced in the 1940s, ejection seats have saved over 10,000 lives. Ejection seats made by one British company alone, called Martin-Baker, have saved over 7000 people.

This Mk16 ejection seat was built by Martin Baker. It is used in both the Eurofighter and the Dassault Rafale military jets. Although it weighs less than a man, the ejection seat can safely eject the pilot from any altitude including ground level. The whole ejection process is incredibly fast. In 0.25 seconds the pilot is out of the aircraft and in under 3 seconds, the main parachute is fully opened.

Parachute container

The straps in the harness are tightened automatically.

Firing handle

Guide rails

Oxygen supply

Leg straps tighten to help secure pilot firmly in seat.

Rocket pack

How ejection seats work

The pilot pulls the firing handle. This sets off a computer-controlled sequence. The seat straps tighten automatically, and all or part of the plane's canopy is fired away.

The pilot's radio and oxygen are disconnected and replaced by emergency ones built into the seat. The ejection gun fires the seat up the guide rails and free of the plane.

Pilot safety

Pilots and aircrew flying military jets need to be well-protected. They are often flying at very high altitudes and need oxygen to breathe. They usually sit on a pack of equipment that contains tools, a life raft, and even food to help them survive if they crash in an isolated place.

When a fast jet makes a tight turn or pulls out of a steep dive, the force of *gravity** presses hard on the pilot. An anti-G suit stops the force from hurting him. It is filled with air and is worn over the flying suit.

The knee parts of the G-suit are cut out to allow the pilot to bend his knees more easily.

This is the oxygen face mask. The ejection seat has 15-20 minutes supply of oxygen on board.

The tinted sun visor protects the pilot from strong glare.

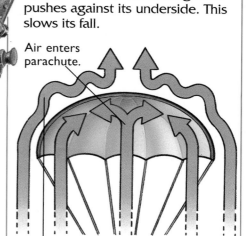

Oxygen supply pipe

These leather gloves are fire-resistant.

The pilot's flying suit and underwear are made from material that is hard to set fire to.

Parachutes

Parachutes slow down a person falling through the air. This means that he or she can land safely when bailing (jumping) out of a plane. A parachute is a large canopy made of flame-resistant material. When open, it creates lots of drag as air pushes against its underside. This slows its fall.

Air enters parachute.

Drag created by catching the air.

Parachutes are tightly fitted into packs either worn by the aircrew or stored on the ejection seat. Sometimes, a second, smaller reserve pack is attached just in case the main one doesn't work.

Parachutes are used for other jobs too. They can slow fast planes down when they land (see page 19). Parachutes are also put on supplies and food so they can be dropped to places without runways or roads.

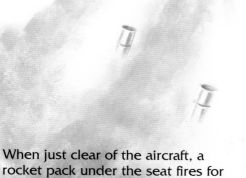

When just clear of the aircraft, a rocket pack under the seat fires for about a fifth of a second. This pushes the seat about 100m (330ft) away from the plane.

An explosive charge opens a small parachute called a drogue. The drogue parachute helps slow the seat down and, on some ejection seats, pulls out the main parachute.

Once the main parachute is deployed, or fully opened, the seat falls away from the pilot who is then left to make an ordinary safe parachute landing.

Modern military planes

This C17 Globemaster transports troops and tanks.

Modern military planes come in all shapes and sizes and perform lots of different jobs. Many of them are designed either to defend an area against an enemy attack or strike at a target with weapons. Not all military aircraft are used just for combat though. Some are used for training, rescue work and transport. Others are used to gather information about an area. This is called reconnaissance. Military reconnaissance planes photograph and check on enemy sites and troop movements.

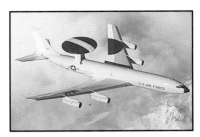

This Boeing AWACS is used for reconnaissance.

Panavia Tornado GR.1

This military jet was built by a group of companies from Germany, Italy and Great Britain. It is used for a number of different tasks and is called a Multi-Role Combat Aircraft (MRCA). This GR.1 version is used mainly as a strike aircraft but also sometimes for reconnaissance.

Here is a GR.1 used by the Royal Air Force in Britain.

This probe collects information about the air and sends it to one of the plane's computers.

This is an air intake. You can see how it is made up of a frame of metal strips all joined together.

The pilot sits at the front. Behind him, the second seat is for the navigator who also operates the weapons.

Cockpit canopy

This radar antenna maps the ground as the Tornado flies along.

The nosecone unhinges to allow engineers to reach the radar equipment stored there.

Inside this pod, advanced electronics and a laser find the distance to a target. It is called a laser rangefinder.

This is the fuel tank of one of the Tornado's missiles.

Swing wings

Straighter wings provide more lift and control which is important for take-off and landing. However, for fast speeds, wings swept back at an angle are best. One solution is to build wings which can swing from one position to another. These are called swing wings.

The Tornado's wings can be moved into one of four different positions, 67°, 58°, 45° and 25°.

67°   58°   45°   25°

The Tornado is a small plane but it weighs more than many bigger aircraft. This is partly because the heavy load it carries. Almost half of the Tornado's weight is fuel and weapons.

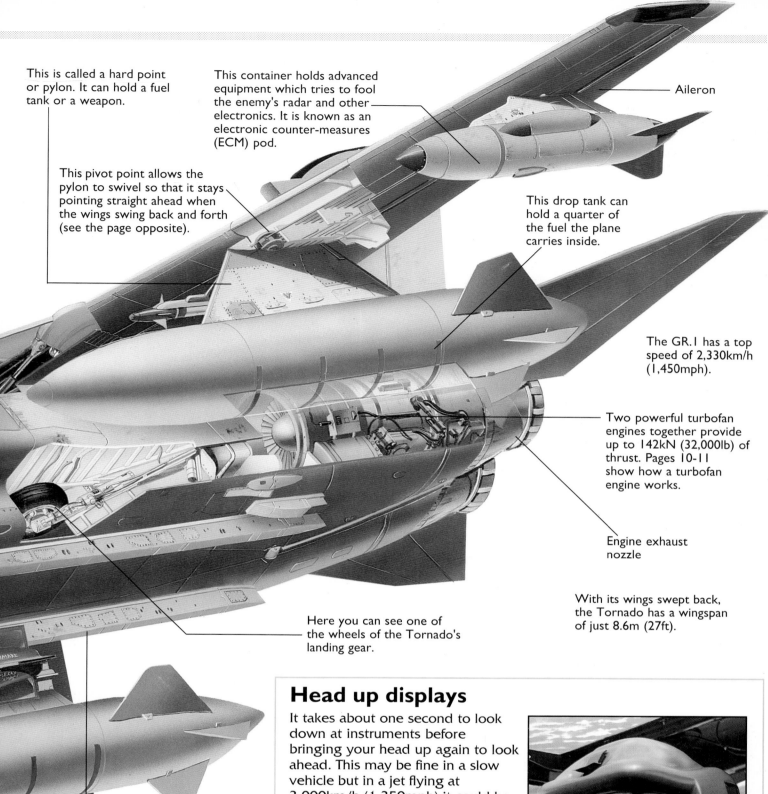

This is called a hard point or pylon. It can hold a fuel tank or a weapon.

This container holds advanced equipment which tries to fool the enemy's radar and other electronics. It is known as an electronic counter-measures (ECM) pod.

Aileron

This pivot point allows the pylon to swivel so that it stays pointing straight ahead when the wings swing back and forth (see the page opposite).

This drop tank can hold a quarter of the fuel the plane carries inside.

The GR.1 has a top speed of 2,330km/h (1,450mph).

Two powerful turbofan engines together provide up to 142kN (32,000lb) of thrust. Pages 10-11 show how a turbofan engine works.

Engine exhaust nozzle

With its wings swept back, the Tornado has a wingspan of just 8.6m (27ft).

Here you can see one of the wheels of the Tornado's landing gear.

Missiles can be launched from these hard points attached to the bottom of the fuselage.

From take-off, the Tornado takes under two minutes to climb to over 9,000m (30,000ft).

Head up displays

It takes about one second to look down at instruments before bringing your head up again to look ahead. This may be fine in a slow vehicle but in a jet flying at 2,000km/h (1,250mph) it could be extremely dangerous. In that time, the plane could have flown over 500m (530 yards).

Head Up Displays, or HUDs for short, are found in many of today's modern military fast jets. They allow information to be displayed straight in front of the pilot either on a clear screen in the cockpit or directly onto the pilot's visor. The screen is see-through so that the pilot can look past the details at the view outside without moving his head.

The projector in this helmet displays important information onto the pilot's helmet visor.

Navigation

The pilots of early planes had little more than maps and a compass to find their way with. They had to plan their course by watching the ground for landmarks. This is called dead reckoning. Today, pilots occasionally use dead reckoning but they usually rely on radio and radar navigation, map computers, and instruments which show the plane's height, speed and heading.

This is a Magellan EG-10 portable electronic map. It can be used in small civil aircraft which don't have expensive map computers built into their cockpit.

Gyroscopes

There are two main devices which help detect a change in the direction of the plane's movement. These are gyroscopes and accelerometers.

A gyroscope used on an aircraft is a fast-spinning wheel joined to a frame. The wheel always stays in exactly the same position, while the frame moves with the plane. The direction and distance that the frame moves is turned into a reading, telling the pilot the change in the aircraft's movement.

Gyroscopes are used in important navigational instruments like the artificial horizon and the directional gyro, which is a type of non-magnetic compass.

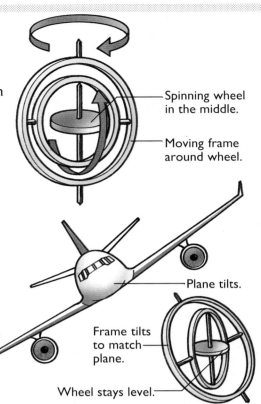

Spinning wheel in the middle.

Moving frame around wheel.

Plane tilts.

Frame tilts to match plane.

Wheel stays level.

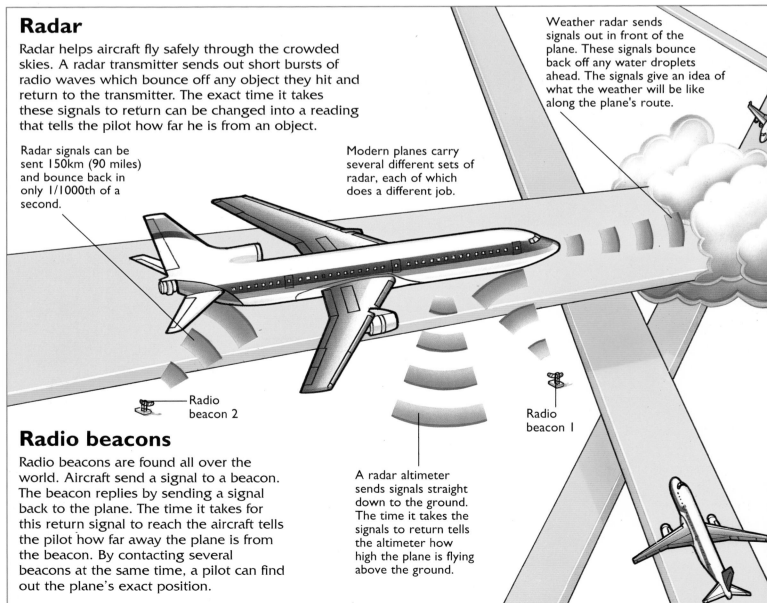

Radar

Radar helps aircraft fly safely through the crowded skies. A radar transmitter sends out short bursts of radio waves which bounce off any object they hit and return to the transmitter. The exact time it takes these signals to return can be changed into a reading that tells the pilot how far he is from an object.

Radar signals can be sent 150km (90 miles) and bounce back in only 1/1000th of a second.

Modern planes carry several different sets of radar, each of which does a different job.

Weather radar sends signals out in front of the plane. These signals bounce back off any water droplets ahead. The signals give an idea of what the weather will be like along the plane's route.

Radio beacon 2

Radio beacon 1

Radio beacons

Radio beacons are found all over the world. Aircraft send a signal to a beacon. The beacon replies by sending a signal back to the plane. The time it takes for this return signal to reach the aircraft tells the pilot how far away the plane is from the beacon. By contacting several beacons at the same time, a pilot can find out the plane's exact position.

A radar altimeter sends signals straight down to the ground. The time it takes the signals to return tells the altimeter how high the plane is flying above the ground.

Accelerometers

An accelerometer is an electronic device which does a similar job to a gyroscope. One part of an accelerometer is in a fixed position and another part can move with the plane. Electricity produces a *magnetic field** between the two parts and any change in movement disturbs the field. This change is fed into a computer which calculates the amount of movement.

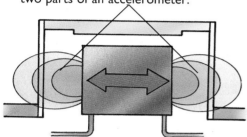

Magnetic fields created between the two parts of an accelerometer.

Autopilot

Most planes today have a system called an autopilot. It allows a plane to stay on a set course without the pilot having to hold the controls all of the time. An autopilot uses accelerometers and gyroscopes to detect movement. If the plane is moving off course, the autopilot's computer triggers electric or hydraulic motors, called servos.

These move the flight controls to bring the plane back on course. If the plane moves a large distance off course, the autopilot also warns the pilot. Autopilots are incredibly accurate, but there are some situations where the pilot's skill and experience are needed and autopilots cannot be used, such as flying through very bad weather.

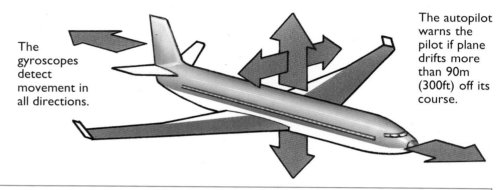

The gyroscopes detect movement in all directions.

The autopilot warns the pilot if plane drifts more than 90m (300ft) off its course.

Air corridors

With so many planes flying, important rules have been made to prevent collisions. Systems of aerial highways, called air corridors, have been created. Each plane flies along one specific corridor a safe distance away from any other planes.

Each corridor is about 15km (9 miles) wide and runs at a certain height above the ground.

There is usually a height difference of 500m (1600ft) between air corridors.

The descent towards the airport runway is called the approach.

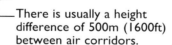

Air traffic control

When flying, the pilot must obey the rules of the air, just as a car driver follows road traffic laws. Air traffic controllers manage aircraft in the skies and advise them on route changes or emergencies. Air traffic controllers use radios to speak to pilots but they also use two systems of radar. The first finds all the planes in the area a controller is scanning. The second receives an automatic signal from each aircraft which gives the controller the plane's identity, height and planned route. As a plane travels out of one area, it is handed from one controller to another.

This is part of air traffic control near London's Heathrow Airport.

Stacking and landing

When a plane gets close to a busy airport, it often has to join what is called a stack. This is like an aerial ladder made up of lots of different levels or rungs. When a plane arrives, it usually joins the stack at the highest point. The plane then travels around an oval-shaped route. Gradually, as aircraft below it land, the plane is ordered down the rungs of the ladder by the air traffic controllers. Eventually, it will reach the bottom level and then begin its approach to land.

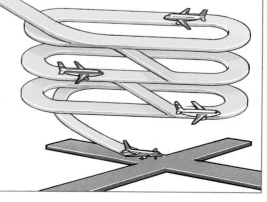

Stealth planes

This is a F117A on a test flight over the United States.

Radar is very successful at spotting aircraft. Recently, engineers have found ways to make it harder for radar to see planes. Aircraft which are built with these anti-radar features are called stealth planes. Stealth confuses an enemy's electronics and radar equipment so the plane can fly by unnoticed. The United States has two stealth planes, the Northrop B2 bomber and the Lockheed F117A strike aircraft.

Here you can see the Northrop B2's shape which is called a flying wing.

Lockheed F117A

This was the first stealth plane to be built and it first flew in 1981. It can travel secretly past heavily-defended enemy sites at night. The F117A is believed not to carry guns or air-to-air missiles. Instead, it relies on its stealth to escape harm.

The cockpit canopy is fitted with treated windows which do not reflect radar signals.

The weapons bay can hold two large laser-guided bombs.

LT COL JERRY CARPENTER

RESCUE

These spikes are called pitot tubes (see page 7).

Air data computers use the information from the pitot tubes.

Infrared light beams can show you things in the dark. This forward-looking infrared machine (known as FLIR) gives the pilot a clear picture at night.

This intake allows air into the engine. It can also be heated to prevent ice from forming in cold weather.

Facets and radar absorbant material (RAM)

What a plane looks like on a radar screen is called its radar cross-section, or RCS for short.

Radar bounces off large curved shapes best. So, instead, stealth planes are built with lots of differently-angled faces or facets. The facets are coated with a mixture of materials (called RAM) which absorb the radar signals rather than letting them bounce off. Together, facets and RAM make a stealth plane look more like birds than an aircraft on a radar screen.

Radar signals bounce smoothly off.

The facets confuse the radar signals which bounce off in all directions.

The R.A.M. coating absorbs many of the radar signals.

On a normal aircraft, radar waves bounce off the large metal surfaces and back to the radar system.

On a stealth aircraft with facets, the signals bounce off at all angles and send back a confusing message to the radar station.

Avoiding the enemy

There are other ways to avoid being seen by the enemy apart from using stealth. Many warplanes since earliest times have been painted in shades and patterns to match the sky or ground, called camouflage. Some very fast jet planes use sheer speed to avoid being seen. Other planes, like the SR71 Blackbird, fly at extremely high altitudes.

The SR71 Blackbird is the fastest jet aircraft ever. Its top speed is over 3500km/h (2180mph).

This Sukhoi Su35 Russian jet fighter is camouflaged to match the winter landscape in Europe.

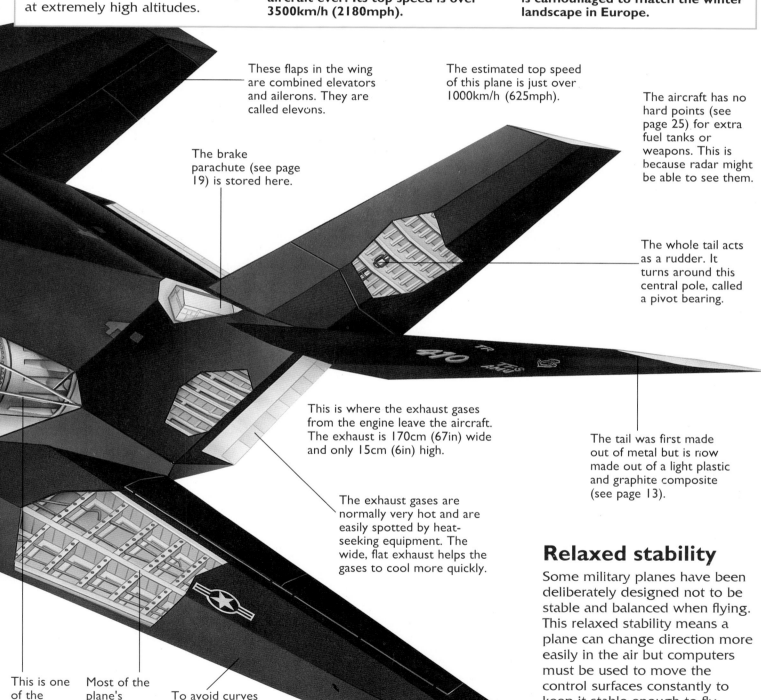

These flaps in the wing are combined elevators and ailerons. They are called elevons.

The estimated top speed of this plane is just over 1000km/h (625mph).

The aircraft has no hard points (see page 25) for extra fuel tanks or weapons. This is because radar might be able to see them.

The brake parachute (see page 19) is stored here.

The whole tail acts as a rudder. It turns around this central pole, called a pivot bearing.

This is where the exhaust gases from the engine leave the aircraft. The exhaust is 170cm (67in) wide and only 15cm (6in) high.

The tail was first made out of metal but is now made out of a light plastic and graphite composite (see page 13).

The exhaust gases are normally very hot and are easily spotted by heat-seeking equipment. The wide, flat exhaust helps the gases to cool more quickly.

Relaxed stability

Some military planes have been deliberately designed not to be stable and balanced when flying. This relaxed stability means a plane can change direction more easily in the air but computers must be used to move the control surfaces constantly to keep it stable enough to fly. Computers on board the F117A make as many as 40 adjustments to the *control surfaces** every second.

This is one of the F117A's two engines.

Most of the plane's structure is made from aluminium.

To avoid curves which reflect radar well, even the edges of the wings are made up of facets.

Navigation light

The future

In less than a century, aircraft have gone from being a dream to having a big impact on our lives. Nobody knows what will happen in another hundred years but it is possible to suggest what may happen in the near future.

Giant airliners

Aircraft makers will continue to look at ways of building airliners which are quieter, use less fuel and which can transport passengers at less cost.

This fuselage has two floors of seats.

This shape is called a clover-leaf body.

More and more people want to travel by air and major airports cannot easily handle lots more flights. One solution is to build bigger airliners. Here are some possible airliner fuselage designs for the future.

This design has two airliner fuselages joined together. It is called a horizontal double bubble.

Airbus A3XX

The Airbus A3XX is a giant airliner planned by Airbus Industries to hold as many as 830 passengers. It would not be much longer than a Boeing 747 but would have a much larger fuselage. There would be two floors for passengers and a bottom deck for cargo. As it will be made using some of the same parts as the Airbus airliners already in service, the A3XX could be flying by the year 2003.

A computer-generated picture of what the A3XX may look like.

Rocket engines

Rocket engines are used for space vehicles but a small number of aircraft such as the fastest ever plane, the Bell X-15, have been powered by rocket engines. Rocket engines are similar to gas turbine or jet engines (see pages 10-11) except that they don't have *turbines** and carry their own supply of oxygen on board.

The Bell X-15's top speed of 7300km/h (4530mph) makes it the fastest ever.

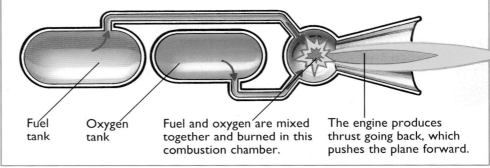

Fuel tank

Oxygen tank

Fuel and oxygen are mixed together and burned in this combustion chamber.

The engine produces thrust going back, which pushes the plane forward.

Space airliner

In the future, you may see airliners powered by a mixture of rocket and jet engines. They would be extremely fast and designed to fly partly in space and partly in the Earth's atmosphere. They would cut down the journey time from one side of the planet to the other to perhaps as little as two or three hours.

This is an artist's impression of a Japanese rocket airliner flying in the 21st century.

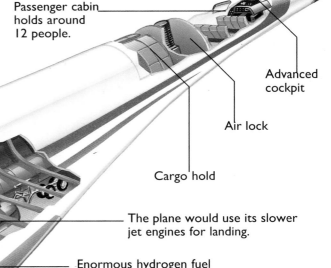

Passenger cabin holds around 12 people.

Advanced cockpit

Air lock

Cargo hold

The plane would use its slower jet engines for landing.

Enormous hydrogen fuel tanks fill most of the plane.

Cruising through space, the high-powered engines could push the plane to speeds as high as 10,000km/h (6200mph).

These powerful rockets would be used for take-off.

Pilotless planes

Electronics and computers will become more advanced and control more and more parts of an aircraft. In the future, pilotless planes could shuttle cargo and passengers from one place to another, guided by navigation systems from the ground.

An artist's idea of what a pilotless plane might look like.

Space cargo carriers

Many companies are working on designs for reusable space vehicles to help or replace the Space Shuttle. The design below, from an American company, Lockheed, has no wings. Instead, it relies on its body to create lift. It would take off like a rocket but land like a normal plane on a runway.

Just over 33m (110ft) long, this craft would carry as much as 500 metric tonnes (550 US tons) of fuel.

Advanced take-off

Many aircraft makers are working on military aircraft with advanced take-off and landing systems. Some are even planning designs for small airliners which could operate from very short runways.

Lockheed's design for a lightweight fighter jet includes a lift fan for very short take-offs and vertical landings.

Glossary

Aerodynamics. The science of how gases, such as air, move over an object. Aerodynamics greatly affect the way planes are designed, built and flown.

Aerofoil. An object shaped to produce lift when air flows over or under it. This shape is most often seen in aircraft wings.

Air pressure. The force with which air pushes against an object. Air pressure is increased by pushing air into a small space. This is called compressing.

Alloys. A metal which is mixed with other metals or substances. For example, steel is an alloy made by mixing iron with carbon. Alloys, particularly of aluminium, are very important in the aircraft industry.

Biplane. An aircraft which has two sets of wings.

Combustion chamber. The part of a gas turbine engine where the air and fuel mixture is set alight.

Compressor. The part of a gas turbine engine where air is squashed together just before it is mixed with fuel and burnt.

Control surfaces. The hinged parts of a plane's wing and tail that help the plane change direction.

Duralumin. A metal alloy (see above) made by adding a small amount of copper to aluminium.

Four forces of flight. The four forces acting on a plane when it flies. The forces are drag, thrust, lift and gravity (see below).

Friction. The resistance made when one surface moves and rubs against another surface and when air moves over a plane.

Fuel management system. A system which adjusts the amount of fuel in each tank and how the tanks supply fuel to the engine or engines.

Galley. The mini kitchen on an airliner where food and drink are prepared for the passengers.

Gravity. A force which pulls objects towards the ground. Gravity has to be overcome by lift from the plane's wings for a plane to rise into the air.

HOTAS. Stands for hands on throttle and stick. Some modern military jets are fitted with an advanced throttle and control column or stick which contains all the controls needed for air combat.

Hydraulics. A system which uses liquid to transmit power from one place to another.

Ignite. To set fire to something.

Inertial Navigation System (INS). An advanced navigation system which measures any changes in the aircraft's speed and direction of movement. The changes are fed into a computer which constantly plots a plane's position. INS is very accurate over long distances.

Mach 1. Mach is a measure of speed. Mach 1 is the speed at which sound travels.

Magnetic field. The area around a magnet that responds to the magnet's power to attract or repel.

Monoplane. An aircraft which has one set of wings.

Pressurization. Keeping the inside of a plane filled with air at a greater air pressure (see above) than the air outside of the plane. This is so that the aircrew and passengers can breathe normally.

Range. The distance an aircraft can travel without running out of fuel.

Stalling. The break up of airflow over the wings caused by not flying fast enough or angling the nose upwards too steeply. Unless corrected, stalling will cause the aircraft to dive dangerously.

Streamlining. To shape an object in a way that makes it move as smoothly as possible through the air. The more easily an aircraft can move, the less power it has to use.

Triplane. An aircraft with three sets of wings.

Turbines. The spinning blades in a gas turbine engine.

Index